Book 1:
Successful Home Based Business Guide
BY JOHN STEVENS

&

Book 2:
The Perfect Interview
BY JOHN STEVENS

Book 1: Successful Home Based Business Guide
BY JOHN STEVENS

Step by Step Strategies, Tips, and Secrets to Starting a Prosperous Home Based Business

Business Box Set #1: Successful Home Based Business Guide & The Perfect Interview

Copyright 2014 by John Stevens - All rights reserved.

In no way is it legal to reproduce, duplicate, or transmit any part of this document in either electronic means or in printed format. Recording of this publication is strictly prohibited and any storage of this document is not allowed unless with written permission from the publisher. All rights reserved.

Business Box Set #1: Successful Home Based Business Guide & The Perfect Interview

Table Of Contents

Introduction 5
Chapter 1 - Build your Entrepreneurial Foundation 6
Chapter 2 - Create a Business Opportunity.. 9
Chapter 3 - Explore Potential Sales 12
Chapter 4 - The Business Set-up 14
Chapter 5 - Establish a Strong Online Presence................................... 17
Chapter 6 - Funding your Business.. 19
Chapter 7 - Design an Efficient Home Office.......................................22
Conclusion 24

Business Box Set #1: Successful Home Based Business Guide & The Perfect Interview

Introduction

I want to thank you and congratulate you for purchasing the book, "Successful Home Based Business Guide: Step by Step Strategies, Tips, and Secrets to Starting a Prosperous Home Based Business."

This book contains proven steps and strategies on how to create a prosperous home based business.

Today's economy has been fluctuating so much that companies are whittling down their pools of local workers and outsourcing their services from abroad instead, which means that true job security is up to you. The best way to survive unemployment is by self-employment, and this book will teach you how to put up and operate your very own business right within the comfort of your own home.

Everyone has the potential to create a self-sustaining business from their personal interests, hobbies, or skills. The most important factor, though, is how to handle the obstacles along the way, balance the financial sheets to prevent (Gasp!) bankruptcy, and consistently improve your business to attract clients and soar above the competition.

The entrepreneurship road is long, but as long as you're equipped with the right know-how, you will be able to reap the rewards.

Thanks again for purchasing this book, I hope you enjoy it!

Business Box Set #1: Successful Home Based Business Guide & The Perfect Interview

Chapter 1 – Build your Entrepreneurial Foundation

Running your own business is the best, albeit not the easiest, way to make a living, and the best place to start is right at home. Once the entrepreneurial bug has bitten you, you will be on a roll to start turning your ideas into actual products and services.

Where to Begin
What should you do first? Before you can answer that question, you must answer this one: What do you want to be?

Let's say you can choose whatever answer you want without any outside influences such as financial constraints or family concerns. Your age does not even matter, because the reality is there is no deadline to ambition. If you are sixty years old and would still want to become a lawyer, then go right ahead and pursue it!

It is also important to fill your mind with positive affirmations and create a mantra, such as "I can do this!" to inspire you to push through with this goal. Many people have plenty of ideas, but they only stay as ideas unless you take the steps to put these ideas into action.

Now, take this very moment as an opportunity to decide on what you want to be. Write it down in big bold letters. The bigger the dream, the better it is.

The next step is to start acting and thinking like the person that you want to be. For instance, if your goal is to become the CEO of a chain of restaurants, you can ask yourself, "How would the CEO of a chain of restaurants deal with this situation?"

Take Baby Steps

Business Box Set #1: Successful Home Based Business Guide & The Perfect Interview

Let your big goal be your guide as you start taking concrete steps on starting your home based business. In other words, what you are doing is breaking down this major goal into smaller and more manageable pieces. In the restaurant chain CEO example, you can start with honing your skills in the food business, and at the same time start advertising made-to-order dishes online.

One essential principle in starting a home based business (or any business for that matter) is delaying gratification, or to sacrifice now and reap greater rewards later. Most people fail at following this principle, which is why they say about 90 percent of businesses fail within the first three years. For example, if you have been an employee for most of your life, you will need to set aside a certain amount of money to help start up your business. Many people cannot do that because they have a certain lifestyle to maintain. But if you choose to push through with your home based business, you know that your sacrifice will take you a long way. Besides, if you worked hard in saving up for your business capital, you will end up being more careful with your business compared to what you'd do if you borrowed money for your start-up.

The Three Building Blocks to a Successful Home based Business

Finally, before you move on to the more specific strategies on starting your home based business, keep these three building blocks in mind: Skills, Network, and Market.

Skills are the fuel that runs your business. Aim to be the best provider of whatever product or service you choose to sell, based on the skills that you have. Aside from that, you must also continue to hone your business skills because no matter how fast your product sells, your business will not grow unless you have accounting, managing, and marketing skills. Of course, you can always hire someone to do this work for you but it never hurts to know the basics yourself.

Networking is another essential building block because it is from here that your business will thrive. As someone who is in business, it is crucial to have the "right connections." Write down all of the people who might be interested in your product, and even those who might not be. Sharpen your interpersonal skills and start getting in touch with them as soon as you have come up with your business plan.

The **Market** is where all of the business takes place. You must find out what your market is so that you can tailor your business to suit their needs. A lot of businesses fail to listen to their market; that is why many products do not sell well. You must learn to adapt to your market and create the need that they are demanding so that your business will become prosperous.

Always go back to these three building blocks whenever you come across an obstacle in your business.

Chapter 2 – Create a Business Opportunity

The first step in creating a business is to turn your idea into a product or service that adds value to your potential market. This idea will become successful if the demand is high and sustainable enough for you to gain sales and earn a profit.

Turn your Idea into a Business Opportunity:
Do you know what product or service to provide? Once you do, there are two aspects that you need to consider: competence and innovation. Let's say you are consistently good at baking large batches of cupcakes; this is your competence. With your baking skills, you came up with a unique set of flavors for cupcakes that you think will sell; this is innovation.

If you are currently employed, look at your company as a place where you can constantly improve your competence, then see how you can establish networks among people and learn the ropes of the company so that you can innovate and come up with even better ways once you have your own business.

If you do not have any ideas yet, then reflect on the crises that people are currently facing. From here, you can come up with an idea that will satisfy a particular need. Let's take a look at some tested and proven examples of crises turned into business opportunities: weight loss recipe books and exercise equipment for obesity, couple therapy for relationships going downhill, pastry shops for those who like to eat cake but do not know how to bake, and so on. From these old ideas, you can innovate and come up with a unique product or service of your own.

Choose your Market
Once you have your business idea, the next step is to determine "who" you are going to sell it to. They are the people whom you need to please so that your product will sell. No matter how great you think your idea is, if nobody would buy

it, your business will fail.

To identify your market, you must first take a look at the demographics (i.e. the age, gender, income, and occupation) of your potential customers. This answers your "who your market is" question. To describe your best customers, you can start by identifying their Life Stage (are they students, young professionals, family starters, or retirees?) and their Income Level based on Occupation (white or blue collar) and Ownership (do they live in apartments, houses, drive their own cars, or take public transportation, etc). Be as specific as you can so that you can start observing your market and finding out their needs and wants.

Next, you should determine the geographics of your market, or the matter of place. Since you will be running a home based business, you have two main fields from which you can get your market: your local area and online. Obviously the latter will provide you with a larger market, but you must also take into consideration the payment process and cost of delivery. Nevertheless, it is best to diversify and cater to both. Your geographics answer the "where your market is" question.

Last, you must measure the psychographics of your market. This includes the behavior of your customers towards your product or service. This is a fun and challenging endeavor as people are naturally idiosyncratic, meaning you cannot please everyone. This aspect answers the question as to "How and Why your market buys from your business." Think about what would motivate them to buy your product. Is your product going to satisfy a basic need (food or shelter), save them time or energy, help boost their self-esteem, or give them pleasure and excitement? You should also answer the following questions: How often will they buy your product? How many products will they buy? How much is your price compared to the competition?

The Niche Strategy
Whatever type of home based business you choose to run, you can still apply the

Business Box Set #1: Successful Home Based Business Guide & The Perfect Interview

Niche Strategy. It is great for start-ups because it means you do not have to compete with the big corporations by lowering your price just to attract buyers. One way to define this strategy is by stating an example:

Let's say you want to start selling cupcakes online, but there are already three other successful cupcake websites in your area. You check out their sites and found out that they sold twice the number of flavors that you sell. You cannot afford to have that many flavors. However, you notice that there is a growing demand for party cupcakes in your area, so you create a special cupcake buffet that includes a "make your own cupcake" corner for parties. You hand out calling cards to families with growing kids and tell them that you not just sell cupcakes, but prepare cupcake buffets for parties." They are more likely to remember to call you once they throw a party because you have chosen your niche.

Chapter 3 – Explore Potential Sales

Now that you have created a business idea and have chosen the suitable market for it, the next step is to estimate the demand or sales of your product or service. In theory, sales is equal to price multiplied by quality multiplied by frequency. To make your home based business a success, you must consider the long term relationship with your customers instead of just the one time deal.

To explore potential sales, the first step is to research on existing competition or anyone else who has already started a home based business that is similar to yours. Most of the time, you will find this information in blogs or on the websites of other businesses. You might even want to send emails to them to inquire about their business.

The information that you will want to obtain from your research are the following: The price and quantity that customers buy, the purchasing habits of the customers (whether they buy in bulk or only in discount), when and how the customers purchase the product or avail of the service (is it in the morning, lunch, evening, weekends, etc?) And how many times within the week do they purchase (and which days are peak or slow)?

Once you have your answers, you can then polish your business to fit the needs of your customers. In other words, your customers should have a compelling reason to buy your product or service despite the competition that has been there before you. Create value for your customer by providing a solution to their problems, and your business will grow.

Creating your Actual Product or Service
Now that you have the necessary information to jumpstart your start-up home based business, the next step is to create your actual product. Always remember the three important things that make a person buy a product: if it satisfies their

physical or basic needs, if it provides solutions to their problems, and if it makes them feel happy.

To finalize your product, go back to your idea and target market. Then determine when, where and with whom they would use the product, why they would use it, and how they use it.

For example, if plan to sell cupcakes, your answers to the "when, where and with whom" questions are: at home and outdoors during parties, with family and friends at the dining room or party place. Your answer to the "why" question is: for desserts or snacks, and the answer to the "how" question is: eat it while enjoying the flavors and toppings. The answers to these probing questions will provide you with a host of specific ideas on how to tailor-fit your product to suit your customers' desires. What colors are best used during parties? What flavors do everyone like? How do you decorate or prepare your cupcakes such that they become "novelty" items in a party? Your ideas will help you stand out from the sea of home based cupcake makers.

Chapter 4 – The Business Set-up

This chapter explains the more challenging part of starting your home based business, and it is about the business set-up. There are two major roles that you will choose from in creating your home based business, and it is to be either the producer or the retailer.

But before continuing, it is a good idea to be familiar with the different business models that you can start with. These are: the manufacturer, the producer, the distributor, the wholesaler, and the retailer.

The manufacturer is the one who manufactures commercial or industrial products such as food, chemicals, clothing, and so on.

The producer is the one who produces agricultural crops or livestock such as wheat, vegetables, fruits, beef, pork, and so on.

The distributor is the one who is involved in storing and distributing the products from the manufacturer or the producer to the point of sale, or the wholesaler and the retailer.

The wholesaler is the one who purchases bulk sales of the products and then repackages them into smaller units to be sold to retailers.

The retailer is the one who sets up a shop in which to sell the smaller units to the consumers.

As you will be starting small, you can start off as a retailer and then work your way up to becoming bigger as soon as you get a sustainable market.

How to Create your Business Set-up

Business Box Set #1: Successful Home Based Business Guide & The Perfect Interview

The easiest way to find out whether or not the business set-up that you have chosen will work is by looking at existing business set-ups made by others before you. Be wary of the pros and cons of each.

It is also important to remember the factors that determine the sustainability of your business set-up, and these are: Time and Effort, Risk Appetite, and Capital. It is imperative that you put the right amount of time and effort that you put into a business especially during the start-up. Watch over your business like a hawk and take time to listen to your customers and always monitor what your market wants.

Capital is a major dilemma of most businesses, especially if you are starting small. While building your home based business from a small capital may take a while, what matters is that you can still manage to get some sleep at night even at the risk of losing your capital.

Risk appetite is just as important as the other two, for this depends upon your ability to face failure and start all over again despite losses. The general advice given to start-up businesses such as home based ones would be to use an existing business model.

Business Set-up Suggestions
Since you're running a home based business, you can start with either of these two suggestions if you have not decided on a particular set-up yet:

Small "own name" shop or office. You can set up a small shop or office at home and then create a website for your online presence. You can also create an exclusively online shop and do the transactions on a computer at home.

Tie-up with an Existing Business. Provide additional products and/or services for current businesses in your area or online. You should protect your products in such a way that they cannot be copied and sold directly by the businesses themselves (In other words, guard your "secret recipe.").

Lastly—and this is very important—ensure your business rights by securing the necessary legal documents. This is to protect your business or practice at home and prevent any problems in the future.

Business Box Set #1: Successful Home Based Business Guide & The Perfect Interview

Chapter 5 – Establish a Strong Online Presence

Since you will be operating a home based business, your primary networking and marketing platform should be no less than the worldwide web. There are plenty of sources out there to guide you on how to create multiple social media accounts and set up an online shop. This chapter is simply dedicated to giving you essential guidelines on where to begin.

Choose social media that suits your target market

There are a lot of social media sites out there which you can use to reach out to your market. These sites include Facebook, Twitter, LinkedIn, Pinterest, and Instagram. Your target market might not be lurking in some of them. While it is still ideal for you to maintain free accounts in all the social networking sites that you can possibly manage, it is important to spend on advertising only in those which cater to your market. Study the cost effectiveness of the Internet marketing campaign that you are about to launch before you actually launch it.

Understand your Market's Online Culture

Nowadays, people who are online rarely purchase products because they scream "buy me!" What attracts netizens to a webpage is the usefulness of the content. To gain the favor of your market and attract them to your shop, you must provide content that is of value to them. With permission, you can share the videos, blog posts, and articles of other people, or you can come up with your own. Your business should be featured as a banner ad or a watermark on your work with a corresponding link that will entice the netizens to click and be directed to the selling page of your website.

Keep your eyes on the prize

No matter how many followers you have gained or how high the click-through rate you have achieved, the one thing that really matters is your sales. The visitors to your website and social media should be enticed to avail of your products or services.

Do not forget the mobile users
More and more netizens have turned to smaller screens as they surf and browse, which means you should create a website or online store that is easy to navigate and fast to load.

Follow the Online Business Trend
There are three essential venues that your business has to have in order to establish a strong online presence. The first is a website that will serve as your "home base". The second is your presence on social media sites to connect your website to your market as well as to keep up with your customers. Last, you need at least one online storefront on sites such as Amazon, eBay, and so on. An additional tip is to list your business where virtual shoppers hang out, such as the local directory Google Places for Business.

Regardless of the type of home based business you are going to run, be it a made-to-order bake shop or a home based psychotherapy or dentist clinic, you absolutely have to be represented online. Think about it: the first thing anyone ever does nowadays when they need to search for something is to Google it and you definitely want to be on top of the search list.

Chapter 6 – Funding your Business

How much money do you really need to start a home based business? The most common excuse that people make as to why they do not turn their business ideas into action is that they do not have the financial resources to fund the start-up.

Alternative Ways to Start your Business without Capital
The truth is, you do not necessarily need money per se to start your business. Aside from money, there are three other ways to fund your entrepreneurial venture: work on commission, become a jobber, go into trading, or using your existing skills and/or talent.

Work on commission. Most real estate brokers, insurance agents, and other pre-need plan salespeople do not have to pay cash for the products or services that they are selling. What they do is to find prospects, market the product or service, and then close the deal to get commissions. As your clientele grows, you can hire and train other salespeople to work under your wing and gain profit from them.

Become a jobber. A jobber is also a salesperson, but in this case, he sells products or services from big merchants and then sells these to retailers. This is also on a commission basis. You will not need money to buy and sell the items as well because you will have a so-called "buyer's credit".

Go into trading. The most popular way to start a business even without capital is to find a supplier who trusts you well enough to provide you with stocks that you can pay on a later time. In fact, many big suppliers support this to help start-up entrepreneurs with their business. Besides, this is an advantage to the supplier as well; he does not need to spend on overhead cost for a brick and mortar shop to sell his goods.

Use existing skills and/or talent. If your goal is to run your own brick and mortar shop someday but you do not have the funding for it yet, then invest on your own skills and talents. If you want to set up a bakery in the future, start selling cupcakes online. Likewise, raise the money for your restaurant by becoming a chef consultant or running a catering service.

How to Find the Needs of your Business

Many newbies in business have the notion that you need to spend a lot of money for equipment, but the reality is you do not really need to buy all of them at once to start producing your product or service. Nevertheless, if you need equipment for your home based business, here are some recommendations:

Borrow. You can also ask to borrow readily available certain equipment that you will need to start your business. There are suppliers who are willing to lend equipment to start-up businesses. All you need to do is to ask.

Buy. In the event that you need to buy certain equipment, haggle for a bargain as much as you can. You can lease certain products first before you buy them, ask for deferred payment and then start paying once your business starts to gain positive cash flow, buy equipment in the form of installment, or buy at a discount or ask for freebies.

Your Business and "Other People's Money"

Many self-help business books usually recommend that you use other people's money to fund your business. However, this only applies to those whose product and/or market are already proven. The only person you can really turn to in financing your home based business is yourself.

Your savings and credit score are the biggest factors that can give you leverage for bank loans; savings in particular will be used as the collateral for the loan. The advantages that you will gain from this is that you will have a lower interest rate because of your collateral, and your return on investment will be greater because

Business Box Set #1: Successful Home Based Business Guide & The Perfect Interview

you will be using someone else's money instead of your own. Furthermore, you will have established a better credit rating for bigger and more important loans in the future.

Chapter 7 – Design an Efficient Home Office

Running a business is not unlike running a tight ship. You need to keep a sharp eye on all the ins and outs of your business. When it all boils down, your business is all about the math.

Of course, this also means you should not mix with your household. Expenses at home should never mingle with business, which means you should not turn to your cash box in case you run out of spare change. You should also avoid using business equipment for personal use as much as you can, save for the computer which is versatile.

The only way to maintain organization while balancing work and home within the same vicinity is to establish an efficient office at home. Here are some tips on how to accomplish that:

Separate the Business User from the Personal User on your computer. Log on to a different user account if you are on business so that you will mentally prepare yourself to focus purely on that while you are at the computer. Your business account should hold only the social media and emails that are related to your business. Be your own boss by avoiding temptation to glance at personal emails that should not be done during "business hours".

Be resourceful with storage. Since your warehouse is also your home, you will do well to install space-saving storage tools for your business paraphernalia. If possible, choose a specific room or corner in your home where all of your business-related items will be stored to prevent them from mingling with personal items. Let everyone at home know that this area is strictly for business and no one should be allowed to enter without permission.

Practice good organizational habits. Avoid clutter like the plague, whether at home or in your home based office. Clutter in the environment also affects your mind, and this will prevent you from becoming productive at the fullest. Create a flow for your paperwork such that it will not pile up, have a regular clean-up session, and store or do away with items that you rarely or never use.

Think ergonomic. Since you will be spending a set amount of hours in your home office, make sure to follow standard ergonomic rules. One rule that many people over look is choosing a comfortable chair that compliments your desk. You should also ensure that your work space has sufficient light (natural, if possible) and air. If you can, paint your office area with a cool, neutral color that is easy on the eyes and does not distract you, such as soft greens, pastel blues, or creams and lemons. The office should also be far from noise and other disturbances that will prevent you from maintaining productivity.

Always remember that maintaining a clean and efficient home office is an important step in boosting your productivity and making your business a success.

Conclusion

Thank you again for purchasing this book!

I hope this book was able to help you to get started on a home based business and grow to become self-sustainable and successfully self-employed.

The next step is to continue polishing your business skills and expanding your networks so that your business will flourish.

Finally, if you enjoyed this book, please take the time to share your thoughts and post a review on Amazon. We do our best to reach out to readers and provide the best value we can. Your positive review will help us achieve that. It'd be greatly appreciated!

Thank you and good luck!

Book 2:
The Perfect Interview
BY JOHN STEVENS

The Most Powerful Tips To Successfully Landing The Job!

Business Box Set #1: Successful Home Based Business Guide & The Perfect Interview

Copyright 2014 by John Stevens - All rights reserved.

In no way is it legal to reproduce, duplicate, or transmit any part of this document in either electronic means or in printed format. Recording of this publication is strictly prohibited and any storage of this document is not allowed unless with written permission from the publisher. All rights reserved.

Business Box Set #1: Successful Home Based Business Guide & The Perfect Interview

Table Of Contents

Introduction 28

Chapter 1 - Preparing for the Interview 29

Chapter 2 - Suit Up! 31

Chapter 3 - Staying Calm during the Interview 33

Chapter 4 - Anticipating the Questions 35

Chapter 5 - Maintaining Rapport and Respect 38

Chapter 6 - Leaving the Best Impression 40

Chapter 7 - What to Avoid 41

Conclusion 42

Business Box Set #1: Successful Home Based Business Guide & The Perfect Interview

Introduction

I want to thank you and congratulate you for purchasing the book, *"The Perfect Interview: The Most Powerful Tips To Successfully Landing The Job!"*

This book contains proven steps and strategies on how to do great in job interviews.

Interviews are usually the most dreaded part of the application process. It is perceived by the companies, on the other hand, as the most efficient means to assess prospective employees.

This book tells you the secrets on how to ace any interview. You will be briefed on how to prepare for the interview, how to maintain your calmness, how to answer specific questions, how to dress, and what things you should avoid. This compendium is written in a very simple manner and the tips are very practical. Hopefully, this will be instrumental for you to get the best life ahead.

Thanks again for purchasing this book, I hope you enjoy it!

Business Box Set #1: Successful Home Based Business Guide & The Perfect Interview

Chapter 1 – Preparing for the Interview

Just like any important personal or professional endeavors, you need to prepare well for that job interview because it will determine the quality of life that you will have ahead of you. In order to sufficiently prepare for that interview, you need to give yourself a lot of time doing the following first:

- Do some research about the role that you are applying for.

- Look into the company history and the dynamics of the organization.

- Create a personal impression on the current dynamics, trends, and affairs that are long the line of your job sector.

- Explore on what the employer is really looking for and assess your personal qualifications.

- List down the possible questions that might be thrown at you during the actual interview.

- Read this book.

In addition to these, you also need to accomplish the following first:

- Do a detailed planning of the schedule and itinerary of the actual interview day. It is important to make sure that you will arrive at the interview venue around ten to fifteen minutes earlier than scheduled. This will give you sufficient time to rest and compose yourself. You have to bring extra cash just in case you need to take a taxi if you got the directions wrong. If possible, print out the map of the office so that you won't get lost. The map can be easily downloaded if you have Internet connection.

- On the night before the interview, you need to decide on what you will wear. For details on what you need to wear, read Chapter 2 of this compendium for the tips.

- Sleep early on the night before. Get sufficient sleep. That way, your mind will be more alert and you can better perform if your mind and body are one hundred percent awake.

Looking back to your University life, there is an office specializing on giving advice for career track formation. They also help by giving practice interviews. If you can no longer go back to the University to avail of this service, you may do any of the following alternatives:

- Anticipate the questions and practice answering them in front of a mirror or with the help of a close friend or a trusted family member. Ask them to give you the most honest form of feedback so that you will know what to improve.

Business Box Set #1: Successful Home Based Business Guide & The Perfect Interview

- Practice your speaking skills in the non-interview context. When you are talking with your doctor, or with the supermarket cashier, try to simulate the interview situation. These are opportunities for practice because they allow you to speak with people that you are unfamiliar with.

- f you find yourself unsuccessful after an interview, ask for their feedbacks and opinions. These will help you draft a list of advice for yourself. This way, you will know what aspects you should change.

- If you have the cash, hire a private tutor to teach you how to act in the context of an interview.

Finally, you need to be familiar of the things that you need to bring to a job interview. The following are some of them:

- Generally, you need not bring anything aside from your Curriculum Vitae (CV), your cover letter, your job descriptions and specifications, and of course, your personal notes.

- Bring the document that serves as your proof that you are invited and scheduled for interview on that day. Usually, this document also lists down the other documents that you have to bring for further assessment. In most cases, employers ask interviewees to bring certificates of examinations and University diploma. These require some time to locate, so you need to make sure that these are well-prepared way before the interview.

- It is worth bringing a notebook and a pen. If you need to give a presentation, be sure to bring a backup copy of the presentation even if you have already emailed it to the company way before.

- If you have your mobile phone with you, either switch it off or put it to silent mode to avoid the hassle.

Business Box Set #1: Successful Home Based Business Guide & The Perfect Interview

Chapter 2 – Suit Up!

Recently, it has been observed by employers that applicants tend to be a bit too "outlandish" in terms of what they wear during the interview. There are a lot of them who show up in their interview wearing they favorite jeans and sweat shirts. There are others who expose their piercings and wear heavy hair wax to maintain the "spikiness" of their hair. Employers even find it more disturbing to see applicants who are chewing gum wearing shirts that are not ironed and pants that are on the brink of falling down. What these applicants do not know is the fact that it is what they wear that resulted to their failure to get their dream jobs.

When showing up for an interview, you need to dress your best. It truly makes a big difference in most cases. Imagine two applicants who are equally qualified and equally skilled. If one of them is dressed to impress and the other is too casual, the employer is compelled to choose the one whose get up is impressive. It seems like he wants the job better than the other.

Most businesses employ a conservative atmosphere. While it may not be perfectly acceptable, appearance does matter in all kinds of businesses. Maybe in other environments, the climate may not be that conservative, so proper decorum might not be regarded as much. But if you are working in the context that you are still courting the employer's attention, it makes perfect sense that you dress well and suit up for your scheduled interview.

Experts say, "when in doubt, dwell on the conservative side." Being conservative is the safest assumption. "Better overdressed rather than underdressed," they all say. If you are a bit overdressed, at least, it is a product of too much preparation. On the other hand, if you are underdressed, it is a manifestation that you failed to prepare. If you are an employer, you would probably know who to favor in such a situation.

The perception on a person is determined by his looks. Fifty five percent of one's valuation of his self-worth and dignity is attributed to his looks. Therefore, one should dress up properly, especially for a job interview.

If you are a lady, the following are the best things to wear:

- A conservative suit which has a solid color
- A blouse that is color coordinated
- Closed shoes
- A bit of jewelry (not too much, please)
- A very neat hairdo that communicates professionalism
- Very little trace of perfume and sparse amount of makeup
- Nails that are clean and manicured
- A briefcase containing your portfolio

On the other hand, the following is the preferred attire for men:

Business Box Set #1: Successful Home Based Business Guide & The Perfect Interview

- A conservative solid colored suit
- Long sleeve shirt, preferably white in color
- A tie that matches your suit and shirt
- Black socks matched with leather shoes
- No jewelry, except the necessary ones (wedding/engagement ring, etc.)
- Professional-looking and very clean hairstyle
- Not too much aftershave because the smell can be distracting
- Trimmed nails
- A briefcase containing your professional portfolio

Chapter 3 – Staying Calm during the Interview

Now, the day of the interview finally came. You have gone a long way already and you have no reason to mess it up. Just stay calm and stick to the belief that things will turn out fine. In order for you to truly stay calm during your session, here are some useful tricks and techniques that will assist you in getting through the experience with flying colors:

Give yourself sufficient relaxation time, so you need to arrive really early. As mentioned earlier, it is always best to be there ten to fifteen minutes before the scheduled interview. That way, you have enough time to "get the feel" of the environment. Sit down, relax, and compose yourself. Breathe in and breathe out so that you can gather the thoughts that you need and eliminate the unnecessary jitters. If you are a bit nervous, just remember that it is not only the company that checks you out; you are also checking out the company. Maintaining that mantra will help you maintain your calmness and confidence.

Assume that this is just a normal yet professional conversation. Again, you are not the only one who is being put to test here. By looking at it as a conversation, you will be more open and more confident to answer the questions being thrown at you. Flash that smile of confidence and it will make a big difference. Be at ease, it is okay to open up and share what you think.

Gather your confidence and positivity. Before the interview, visualize that "perfect ten" performance. Imagine yourself responding to all questions confidently and impressively. Of course, in the actual interview, you might find yourself with shaking hands or unstable voice. In such moments, just remember that it is okay to stop for a few seconds, take a few deep breaths and proceed with renewed calm. Remember, you are invited to do the interview because someone saw your CV and he thinks that you might do well. That alone is enough reason to celebrate, because someone knew that you have what it takes. So, you should not be nervous. You will do well if you choose to do well. You can do great if you choose to do great.

The interviewer is not a prosecutor. Look at him as a friend. If you will see him as a foe, then you are definitely in trouble. You will have the hostile tendency and you might not be able to respond to his questions in the most logical manner possible. If you want to be treated pleasantly, give your interviewer sufficient reason to treat you as such. He is not a machine created to reject unworthy applicants. Rather, he is also a human being doing his job.

Do not fiddle around. Just sit up steady and straight. Try to maintain this formal stance throughout the interview because it helps in maintaining your confidence and in the projection of your voice. Proper posture helps you exude confidence even if you are really trembling.

Never show that you are stressed by the interview situation. Show that you are capable of being graceful despite the pressure. This way, your interviewer will see you as a person who can take on any challenge. And that's a big plus.

Focus on your personal purpose and back it up with your inherent strengths. Do not be anxious because it will make you feel that your purpose may not measure up or your strengths might not be worthy of comparison. At any point during the interview, do not panic. With the clear purpose in mind backed up by your professional skills, you will be able to get through the interview successfully.

Take your time and normalize your breathing. Remember, you do not have to answer the question the moment the interviewer finishes his question. You can respond after 5 to 10 seconds and that is more than enough to gather your thoughts and formulate your response. Take a deep breath because it drives more oxygen into your bloodstream. The oxygen can help you feel more relaxed.

Do not pretend that you are perfect. Never be disappointed if at any point, you commit a mistake. Remember, employers know for a fact that there exist no perfect employees, so you do not really have to be one. Admit instances when you made mistakes in the past. That will create a very good impression because it shows that you have the sense of responsibility and accountability.

Finally, you need to think of this: the interview that you are having is just one of your many options. There are many other jobs that are available out there. Do not pressure yourself that much to the point of breaking. By adopting this kind of thinking, you will maintain a calm stance and you will not worry that much. Constantly remind yourself that there are other jobs waiting for you out there.

Chapter 4 – Anticipating the Questions

First, you have to ask yourself: "What questions commonly appear in interviews?" The interview process is a mechanism by which employers get to know their prospects. They ask for information that are not written on your CVs so that they will know what to expect and what not to expect from you. The process is two-way. In the interview, it is not only the employer that should do the assessment. You, the applicant, should also get the feel of the work atmosphere.

Many applicants fail big time because they do not get to anticipate the interview questions that are thrown at them. Surprised, they are caught off guard and the next tendency is to panic. When panic strikes, the entire interview is anticipated to be a great mess. To avoid this scenario, just read this chapter and prepare for the questions.

Here are some of the questions that are likely to be covered:
- academic achievements and diplomas or certifications earned
- work background experiences
- interpersonal skills like leadership capability
- personal and professional goals
- personal and professional skills
- career objectives
- how well you understand the role
- personal strengths
- personal weaknesses

Other forms of questions are the following:
- What decisions led to your choice of academic institution?
- What are the most challenging parts of your previous job?
- In what particular scenario were you able to show your effectiveness as a team player?
- What are your reasons for leaving your previous job?
- Give a five-year plan in terms of how you will develop your career.
- What skills and capabilities are you most proud of?
- How can you be of use to the company?
- What is your biggest achievement in life?

- That challenges do you anticipate in this particular job that you are applying for?

Never assume that the interviewer has done his homework – most interviewers do not read the CVs at all. So you need to supply as much information as possible so that you will create the right impression. The responses should be packaged in such a way that your interviewer has no clue of who you are, how much you have achieved, and where you intend to lead your life.

If you find challenging questions in the interview, there are options that are ready for you. Such questions are usually given to determine if you can act appropriately despite the pressure. Here are some tips:

- Prepare well for questions that you can anticipate

- Admit your limitation or lack of knowledge – it is much better that waffling or lying

- When your opinion is asked, do not be too radical or too conservative

- To illustrate your point, try your best to provide examples

- Never assume that your interviewer has an "expected set of answers"

If things get a bit too personal, remember that you can respectfully decline answering the interviewer's question. You can do this if you think that the question is not at all connected to your application for the job.

On the other hand, if it will affect your manner of fulfillment of the role, provide an appropriate response. Do not give out unnecessary information especially if it will jeopardize your safety and privacy.

There are instances, however, when the interview is done in groups. You should be prepared for such a scenario so that you will stand out and be more than just a face in the crowd. What should be expected in group interviews?

- Discussions with other candidates wherein the facilitator and interviewer will ask them to complete a certain task or discuss a certain topic

- A common question for everyone and the candidates will take turn answering

Group interviews are commonly done by companies that believe in the importance of group interactions. Such kinds of interviews are opportunities to manifest your strengths. The following are usually expected from the candidates:

- To be able to show that they have sufficient working knowledge of the given topic

- To demonstrate the capability to take turns, listen to other people's points of view, and understand their points accordingly

- To show that you have the capacity to act as a leader and give a point of convergence for a diverse group of applicants

- To do positive intervention if there are dominant group members
- To summarize the activity or build consensus among different group members

Remember, there are principles that you have to remember in group interviews. First, learn to elaborate. You need to know how to supply relevant illustrations and useful examples. In addition, you have to know how to come up with feasible alternatives. A good team player would know another approach in reaching a desired end. Next, summarization is a desired skill. Remember to include even the points you do not agree with. Lastly, a good team player is an inclusive person. One should be "others" oriented.

Given the chance to ask a question to the one who interviews you, you should have two to three in mind. Here are the most intelligent ones:

- What sort of professional and personal trainings may be expected from the company?
- What expansion plans do the organization intend to engage in the future?
- If ever lucky enough to be accepted, when should I start reporting for duty?

Having these questions in mind and preparing questions show your level of eagerness and genuine passion to take on the role offered by the company.

Chapter 5 – Maintaining Rapport and Respect

Prior conversations can be of help, but in the context of an interview, it is most likely that you will be talking with someone you have just met for a period of twenty minutes or so. According to experts, you need to maximize the meanings that are transmitted by both your words and the actions that go with them.

Rapport is created with the help of the subconscious. It is primarily assisted by non-verbal signs. Among the signals that usually figure in the list are the following: positioning of the body parts, the movement and rhythm of the body, the level of eye contact, the kind of facial expression, and the tone of the voice.

The best illustration here is when you are talking with a close friend. After a minute or two, if you will look closely and pay attention to your non-verbal cues, the tendency is for each of you to copy each other's gestures, movements, and facial expressions, among others. Rapport is usually created in a natural and instinctive manner. It acts as our line of defense against possible conflicts. Throughout the history of mankind, it is quite clear that rapport is effective in maintaining day-to-day peace and harmony.

During an interview, it is important to build rapport with the interviewer. To do this, you need to appropriately use your body language. Be aware of the signs that you are sending and be conscious of the signals being sent by your interviewer. The non-verbal communication should be parallel to the verbal communication. That way, you will appear more pleasant, prepared, open, and relaxed.

When your interviewer is saying something, try to reflect back and clarify whenever there arises any difficulty. This will help you in showing that you are listening closely. Additionally, you will appear more empathic and sensitive.

Also, you have to be careful in using your voice. Project it properly. Deliver what you wish to say in such a way that it reflects your genuine interest. Also, try to stabilize your tone and hide the tense of nervous feeling. It is best to take your time when speaking. Talking quickly will only make you appear stressed or nervous or tense. Furthermore, you can always adjust your pitch, tone, pace, and volume to suit your intention.

There are other behaviors that prove to be helpful in building rapport. Here are some of the following:

- When seated and you wish to project that you are truly interested in what the interviewer is saying, try leaning forward a bit. The hands should be open and the legs and the arms of the person should not be crossed. This kind of non-verbal cue will not only send the message that you are truly listening. This will also help you feel a bit more relaxed.

- Establish eye contact, but do not overdo it. The optimal value would be look at the one you are speaking with around sixty percent of the time. Overdoing this will make your interviewer feel uncomfortable. Meanwhile, doing it less than 60 percent of the time might make your interviewer feel that you are not listening or that you are not paying attention.

- Maintain that sweet smile throughout the interview.

- Remember your interviewer's name. Addressing him using his name will make him feel a bit more important. It is a recognition that you are capable of being respectful.
- When asking questions, choose open-ended ones. Open-ended questions are questions that require well-thought of answers or responses. They are not your typical "yes or no" questions.
- Offer feedbacks to show that you can summarize or reflect on what the interviewer is saying. Aside from building rapport, this will help in clarifying any misunderstandings even before they get bigger.
- Use previous statements given by the interviewer in your answers to show that you are truly listening.
- Even if you are just a mere interviewee, try to show empathy. This can be demonstrated by expressing your understanding of how your interviewee feels on certain issues or matters.
- When you do not know the answer, say it directly. Never pretend that you know the answer or do not try to lie just to come up with an answer. Admitting mistakes is one of the most interesting and most admirable things that an applicant can do.

These will work well if you will try to be more genuine. You may also offer a compliment if it is well-deserved. Finally, maintain your politeness.

Chapter 6 – Leaving the Best Impression

The old saying got it right: "First impressions are the ones that usually last." And in the context of business, these first impressions are the key for maintaining and furthering relationships in business. Your manner of behavior during your interview will be a good determinant on whether you will get the job that you want.

To leave the best impression, here are some tips that you can use:

- Do your homework and research about the company and the job so that you will appear truly interested and knowledgeable. This way, you will appear more confident and your interviewer will surely notice how much you have prepared for your moment. You may get information from the company's website. Their previous press releases and the reviews provided by Google prove to be truly useful as well.

- Be firm when it comes to doing the handshake. A firm handshake is an indicator of determination and perseverance. If your handshake is impressive, you will leave a truly lasting impression.

- Filter words like "um" and "like" should be avoided because they will give away the fact that you are nervous.

- Before you go, try to remind the interviewer about yourself by flashing your smile. You may shake the interviewer's hand once again and walk out of the room with all the confidence that is due.

Also, you need to maintain your eye contact. There's no point panicking. Just relax. It will create an impression that you can truly act under pressure. Finally, you should be the one who know your qualifications best. You should be able to discuss your achievements and aspirations really well.

Some people might, in principle, disagree with the saying "First impressions last." In the context of life, this might not be the case. But in the case of businesses and the workplace, it is true majority of the time. Remember, the interview might be your last chance to show what you've got. In order to avoid regrets, be your best and act your best during the interview.

Chapter 7 – What to Avoid

This chapter is devoted to the things that you have to avoid during any job interview. This will complete your knowledge and it will increase your chances of landing your dream job.
Sometimes, it is not enough to show that you are knowledgeable, skilled, and intelligent. You should also show that you have positive characteristics. There are very intelligent people who fail miserably because of the following:

- Dressing in a very inappropriate manner. There are people who wear shorts or rugged jeans during interview. And they wonder why they are not getting the job. Casual get up is often decoded as not being serious with the application.

- Showing your bad side. If the interview has already begun, by all means avoid peeking at your Android phone. The interview will only cost you 20 minutes of your time or even less. So, do not answer the phone call or the SMS just yet.

- Saying the worst things about your previous employer. Why would a company want an employee who will quit the job and badmouth their previous employer to their next one? Remember, this world is too small for such kinds of people.

- Airing complaints. Interviews are meant to show your positive side. If you will say your complaints about the traffic or the weather, or what-have-you, then you are risking your chance of getting the job. Piece of advice, do not start stepping with your wrong foot or start singing with the wrong tone.

- Being late. Human Resource personnel usually follow a tight schedule during interview days. You should understand that if you come in late, you already forfeit your chance of being assessed.

- Being too personal. As mentioned in the previous chapter, you may decline questions about your personal life, especially if they are not connected with the way you will carry out your duty. Unless you are asked, do not mention anything about your personal life.

- Not showing interest. For example, if you are instructed to ask questions, by all means ask. Not being able to come up with questions is an indicator that you are not really interested.

With the current state of our worldwide economy, you should not risk your chance of getting that dream job. Learn what you need to do and remind yourself of the things that you should not do. That way, you will ace any interview and you will have the privilege to choose your perfect job.
All the best and we hope that you get that job that you are applying for.

Conclusion

Thank you again for purchasing this book!
I hope this book was able to help you to ace any job interview that you are invited to attend. Hopefully, this book will also be instrumental for you to get your dream job.
The next step is to practice these and attend as many interviews as you can!
Finally, if you enjoyed this book, please take the time to share your thoughts and post a review on Amazon. We do our best to reach out to readers and provide the best value we can. Your positive review will help us achieve that. It'd be greatly appreciated!
Thank you and good luck!

www.ingramcontent.com/pod-product-compliance
Lightning Source LLC
Chambersburg PA
CBHW070719180526
45167CB00004B/1542